My Favorite Sports

I LOVE SOCCER

By Ryan Nagelhout

Gareth Stevens
PUBLISHING

Please visit our website, www.garethstevens.com. For a free color catalog of all our high-quality books, call toll free 1-800-542-2595 or fax 1-877-542-2596.

Library of Congress Cataloging-in-Publication Data

Nagelhout, Ryan.
I love soccer / by Ryan Nagelhout.
p. cm. — (My favorite sports)
Includes index.
ISBN 978-1-4824-0735-8 (pbk.)
ISBN 978-1-4824-0772-3 (6-pack)
ISBN 978-1-4824-0734-1 (library binding)
1. Soccer — Juvenile literature. I. Nagelhout, Ryan. II. Title.
GV943.25 N34 2015
796.334—d23

First Edition

Published in 2015 by
Gareth Stevens Publishing
111 East 14th Street, Suite 349
New York, NY 10003

Editor: Ryan Nagelhout
Designer: Nick Domiano

Photo credits: Cover, p. 1 Fuse/Thinstock.com; pp. 5, 15, 23 Monkey Business Images/Shutterstock.com; pp. 7, 9, 19, 21 (soccer ball) Dan Thornberg/Shutterstock.com; pp. 7, 9, 19, 21, 24 (net) Fotokostic/Thinkstock.com; p. 11, 24 (pitch) romakoma/Shutterstock.com; p. 13, 24 (cleats) Stockbyte/Shutterstock.com; p. 17 Alexey Losevich/Shutterstock.com.

Printed in the United States of America

CPSIA compliance information: Batch #CS15GS: For further information contact Gareth Stevens, New York, New York at 1-800-542-2595.

Contents

Soccer is a lot of fun.

I love to run.

I run all over the field.

The field is also called a pitch.

I wear soccer shoes.
These are called cleats.

We play with a
soccer ball. It is
black and white.

I can kick it far.

17

I pass the ball
to my friend.

He kicks it into the net.
This is a goal!

Come play soccer with us!

23

Words to Know

cleats   net   pitch

Index